SERVE THEM RIGHT
A Guide to British Customer Service

Harbour Books Ltd
20 Castlegate
York YO1 9RP
www.harbourbooks.co.uk

Represented in Great Britain & Ireland by
Signature Book Services

First published in Great Britain by
Harbour Books 2005
Copyright © Gregor Poppleton 2005
Illustrations copyright © Steve Chadburn 2005

A catalogue record for this book is available from the British Library.

ISBN 1905128010

Layout by Slabmedia

Printed in Finland by WS Bookwell

SERVE THEM RIGHT
A Guide to British Customer Service

GREGOR POPPLETON
Illustrated by Steve Chadburn

This book is dedicated to those
soldiers of the High Street, the sales assistants.
And to anyone who has ever carried a price gun.

Long Overdue

Generally, the science and art that lies behind retail customer service is a mystery to the public. This is not necessarily a bad thing.

Just as a person may happily travel in a lift without knowledge of the hydraulic mechanisms that enable the lift to function, or run for a bus without worrying too much about the changes in their own cardiovascular system, so it is not a prerequisite of shopping to understand the complex mechanics of customer service — if you want to buy a bucket, you want to buy a bucket. As long as you're in the right shop, have the money to pay for the bucket and know the word for 'bucket' in the country in which you're in, you're three-quarters there. There may be a little discussion over size or whether you want a steel, aluminium or plastic bucket, or if it is for jam making or milking or for general household use, but the point remains: your primary concern is not the service you receive but the bucket.

So, by and large, there's no reason for this book. Most of the world neither needs, nor wants, to know about the ropes and pulleys at work behind the retail experience.

In Britain however the situation is different. For many years it has been a peculiar trait of the British to criticise the customer service they receive in stores as being indifferent, or even rude. This criticism is now so entrenched as to be accepted as fact. It is nothing of the sort. British customer service is a multi-layered, complex structure, far more developed than that of any other country. Sadly though, as it has developed it has left behind the British public, who have no conception of the psychological fine-edges of it and, like the uncouth, disparage what they don't understand. The rest of the world, following the British public's line, now too believes that British customer service is poor.

This book was inspired by a desire to right that wrong and to reveal the truth behind our customer service. British retail has long been too modest or possibly too secretive about its conceptual framework, fearing perhaps it will daunt people of modest abilities from entering the profession. Revealing this framework, however, is the price we must pay to restore to our nation of shopkeepers the respect they deserve for their dizzying, yet mostly misunderstood, wealth of skills.

When we talk about Britain, so often our broad brush paints Ireland, our closest neighbour, in the same colours. It should be made clear therefore that this book deals only with British customer service. For a take on Irish customer service you will have to wait for another book, or write one. It should be mentioned though that the customer service in Dublin or Cork is as developed or, arguably, even more developed than in Britain. Nothing in this book would be unfamiliar to anyone who has ever stepped into an Irish city store.

There will be sales assistants who will be disgruntled that this book has been published; people who would have preferred the art of their profession to remain undisclosed. To these people I apologise. My defence is that with the publication of this book the sales people of Britain will find themselves regarded in a truer, kinder light, and be seen as professionals, such as doctors, lawyers, teachers and firemen, and will at last be granted their due respect — or, to be more accurate, their long overdue respect.

All of this, needless to say, depends on this book gaining wide distribution.

It is, therefore, in every sales assistant's interest to promote this book with ingenuity, purpose and vigour; to ensure – no matter what sector of the retail trade they inhabit – that copies are piled up obtrusively throughout their store; and to let no customer depart without giving them the opportunity to understand the subtle, difficult, truly British science of retail service through the purchase of this book.

Opening Times

Just as we find the arcane opening times of shops in the Mediterranean impossible to decipher or predict, so visitors to this country often have difficulty understanding the opening hours of our establishments.

It is easy to see how this cultural confusion arises. A shop that advertises its opening hour as nine o'clock and opens its doors at that time or thereabouts, might at first glance appear to be inviting customers inside. This, as we know, is not the case.

Our custom of opening shops fifteen minutes before actual trading is to allow staff some time to adjust gradually from the personal to the commercial, to acclimatize themselves to the shopfloor before the business of the day begins. This is what is known in the trade as 'drowsing time': a time for staff to prepare their till floats, nurse cups of coffee, compare television viewing or to nip out to buy pastries. That it exists is a mark of how civilised a country Britain can still claim to be.

When this convention is explained to visitors to the country, they feel foolish for not realising sooner — once brought to their attention it seems so obvious! It explains the curt greetings, the reluctance to help, the hoovering around their feet — the general sense that they are not welcome.

Likewise, they understand that one should not, under any circumstances, attempt purchases from a shop in the last fifteen minutes of the day, this being the staff's other 'drowsing time'.

Counter Intuitive

It is important that sales staff resist putting customers in a position where they might behave, inadvertantly, in an ill-mannered fashion.

Cutting off abruptly the, say, intricate human story you are explaining to your colleague, or to a friend on the phone, just because a customer approaches you, might make the customer think they've interrupted you.

Truncating your story by declining to use the essential 'then he said' and 'then she said' signposts, risks giving the customer the impression that they're badgering you.

The correct response is, unhurriedly, to finish your conversation. In this way you selflessly shield your customer from feelings of behaving badly.

Recognising the Customer

In the past few years there has been some argument as to whether it is better to acknowledge the customer's presence and then continue your conversation with a colleague, or whether it is wiser to take the atheistic approach and deny their existence entirely. Both actions have their merits.

My own view has changed over time. For many years I thought that the better approach was to acknowledge the customer. In this way, the customer was reassured that they had put themselves, so to speak, on your Things To Do list. They could relax in the knowledge that it would only be a matter of time before they received help.

Indeed, as an increasing number of graduates enter the retail environment, bringing with them new skills of concise narration honed from writing one page essays, customers in some areas of the industry have to wait less time than ever to be served.

Despite this, I now believe acknowledgement of the customer is in no one's interest.

It has been found that acknowledged customers lose all initiative to seek out other, more readied, assistance. An acknowledgement creates a form of extreme autism, where customers will stand for long periods, anxious and hyper-ventilitating, waiting for a preoccupied assistant rather than walk a short distance where another assistant might provide them with service.

Customers must be protected from falling into this behavioural dysfunction. Give them no reason to believe you're aware of their existence.

Manners

Remember good manners are everything in the service industry. Treat your colleagues with respect: colleagues who respect one another can, eventually, respect their customers.

Try greeting your colleagues with the words, 'Good morning' or 'Hello'. If they hand you something, risk a 'Thank you'. Should they leave the building, try a 'Goodbye'.

Once you're able to do this, have a go using the same words in your dealings with customers!

If you're one of those assistants who, even after practising on their colleagues, still finds the knack of being consistently polite to customers escapes you, do not despair.

There is more than one way to skin a rabbit.

Whether or not you've ever visited France, always try and introduce into conversation the topic of how legendarily impolite French shop assistants are. Although wholly untrue, their ubiquitously perceived rudeness will, in comparison, make customers think better of your charm-shaved manner.

A Political Stand

It is one of the most unfortunate aspects of the retail trade in this country that there is, as yet, no legislation requiring establishments to provide their salespeople with stools.

Some enlightened establishments do of course make stools available. Others expect their sales staff to cope without stools, to stand behind a till for lengthy periods without any support, save that that they get from leaning against the counter.

If you are a sales assistant in such an establishment, you should bring your plight to the attention of customers. The provision of a stool is a basic need for any shop worker.

As a customer enters your store, let them know by your lemon-lipped demeanour that you have no stool and the last thing you are going to do is ally yourself with this unacceptable practice of capitalism — or indeed any practice of capitalism.

If you work in an establishment that is blessed with stools, show solidarity to your unluckier colleagues, and act in the same way.

Dealing with Till Queues

Those new to the retail trade often believe that taking money from customers at the till is of high importance, central to the well-being of the business. Experienced assistants avoid this type of over-simple theorising. They hardly ever step behind the till, and when they do they ensure that they leave it as soon as possible to do the

essential job of maintaining an ordered shop floor — even when there are people waiting to be served. If you're behind the till and you remember an important job to be done on the shopfloor... simply close your till and walk away. Novices at first may be intimidated by the glowering people waiting in the queue. This is understandable. But don't worry; with experience you will hardly notice them.

Working the Till

These days any one using the term 'multi-tasking' in business is considered to be clowning about.

'Multi-tasking', on the whole, has been discarded, thrown onto the towering scrap heap of worn-out management approaches. Here it has joined the other casualties of the recent past: 'empowerment', 'here to help', 'the customer is always right' and one that for some time looked like it might survive, 'smiling'.

If your store has discarded multi-tasking and you're now tied to the till, you may have a desire to create for yourself a more roving role in the store. Following a few simple rules will ensure that your supervisor reassesses your position behind the till.

Whenever a customer buys five or fewer items ask, 'Would you like a bag with that?'

If more than five items? Wait for them to ask for a bag.

Give the customer the wrong change and then scowl at them when they point out the error. Give them the correct change as though you've been duped.

When a customer hands you a banknote, take the note using the best-not-to-even-think-where-it-could-have-been grip – that is, just the forefinger and thumb.

When giving change, place the receipt in the customer's hand with banknotes on top and then change on top of that. The 'Tower of Pisa' is especially effective if the customer is already balancing shopping in their hands.

Always ask the customer if they want their receipt. Given that it has already been printed and has no value outside of the customer's possession, and given that it would be easier to drop the receipt into their bag, this might seem a too obviously irritating question. Still, as most of your customers will have been brought up firmly in the British comedic tradition, they won't recognise it as such.

If the customer has their picture on their credit card, always ask incredulously, 'Is that you?'

Finally as the customer leaves, make sure you say nonsensically, 'See you later'.

If by chance the customer does return, always act as if you've never seen them before, even though they make purchases from you three to four times a week.

Supermarket Till

Many people are drawn to the position of supermarket cashier because it gives them the chance to operate the conveyor belt — one of the few hand-eye co-ordinated tasks in the world of retail.

But there are other aspects to the job that demand skills that are just as specialised. That other staff frequently overlook these is a source of friction in many stores.

For example, the ability to extemporise on every item as it passes over the scanner is a difficult and mentally demanding task. It is a credit to their creativity that they make it look so easy...

Celeriac (I wouldn't know what to do with it. My husband/ kids would never eat it anyway.)... shoe polish (We hardly sell any of this anymore — who cleans shoes these days)...

steak (So expensive — buy one and half your wage is gone)... oven chips (I go through bags of these at home — we're all too lazy to make the real things aren't we?)... baguettes (We've started having them as a bit of a treat. Can't beat a sliced white though can you?)...

Should you come across an item that is potentially embarrassing, obviously it is best not to comment. Just pass the cranberry juice/emollient cream/earwax remover/mouthwash/large tube of lubricant across the scanner without comment, but with an understanding smile. Sometimes, too, a small shrug might not be out of place.

Ideally you should try to spot any embarrassing item as it approaches on the conveyor belt — before picking it up to scan. In which case, to save the customer embarrassment, you should immediately close the till, robustly informing all the other customers in the queue that your till is closing and they should join the queue of another cashier. By this type of quick-thinking diplomacy, customer discomfort can be minimised.

Communication

Every industry is only as good as its channels of communication. With the revolution in technology providing retail establishments with options such as short-wave radios and intranet networks to facilitate contact

between staff, it is to the industry's credit that it has stuck with a proven form of communication: voice projection. Or, as it is known in store, 'checking'.

It is sometimes forgotten how ingenious a method of communication 'checking' is. If a customer has, say, a stock query that a sales assistant can't answer, the sales assistant 'checks' with another member of staff whether the item is in stock. For 'checking' to be effective two simple rules must be followed. The other member of staff must be at least one communication chain (twenty-two yards) distant, and the member of staff checking must use a volume loud enough for a person standing three times that distance away to hear. The reason for this is simple.

It may just be that the colleague you're asking knows the answer to your query, but more often than not your query will be answered by another colleague, popping up from nowhere, or answering but remaining unseen. The greater the range of your enquiry, the greater the number of people who have the chance to offer an answer. A frequent outcome is that the query is answered by a helpful customer, albeit incorrectly — but the system makes no claim to be authoritative.

Rather, 'checking' is a collaborative, decentralised system involving anyone in the store within earshot who has a contribution to make to the solution of an enquiry. In many ways it is not unlike the early internet in its simplicity and inclusivity, bridging the barrier of distance, allowing people to share information and to work together for a common good.

Whether or not it will evolve like the internet to become an instrument of social and political import remains to be seen. My own view is that it probably won't.

Engaging Your Customer

Avoid eye contact at all times. The eyes are the window to the soul. It goes without saying that few customers would be happy to find you peering in.

If you have difficulty in keeping your eyes averted, try instead to focus on a point just over the shoulder of the customer. This removes any hint of embarrassing eye contact. The disadvantage of this strategy however is that it does tend to slow down transactions; the customer will keep looking over their shoulder to see what you're looking at. This is unavoidable. Having a customer depart with a residue of paranoia is a reasonable price to pay if we are to avoid embarrassing them by over engagement.

The Art of Conversation

Remember customers like nothing more than to hear your opinion on house prices, the economy, car ownership and farming subsidies.

If you run out of pertinent points to make on any of these, then bring the conversation back to yourself. No one has ever been able to explain why customers have such an unquenchable desire to know more about the domestic situation and aspirations of the person serving them, but they do. Anything interesting happened to you recently that you thought hilarious or eerie or that *really* made you think about life? Thought of a new career direction? Met the author of the book your customer is buying and found them insufferable? Let your customer know.

Using Bags

If you find yourself with a 'chatterer', it is polite to talk about the things they talk about, even if you have no interest in the subject.

The optimum length for such a conversation should be sixty seconds or four replies from the assistant — whichever comes first. Anything over this may encourage the customer to think that you've a genuine interest in what they are talking about or, worse, in them.

It is therefore sometimes necessary to cut off a conversation abruptly, even one that you started. Obviously the customer must not think you rude. The best method therefore is to take the customer's purchase and relentlessly attempt to put it into a bag too small for it. The conversation will magically dissolve as the customer watches you struggle. If the customer suggests using a larger bag, thank them but reply that you're sure it *will* fit.

The Silent Approach

There's enough clutter in all our lives, which is why the most perfect retail transaction is one done without words. Such an approach, however, is best left to only the most preternaturally talented young salespeople.

Frequently these retail *wunderkinds* have no inclination to use words at all. From their arrival at work to their departure at the end of the day, all their tasks are done in a mood of meditative calm. They create around them a marvellously tranquil aura, calming the often frayed atmosphere of a busy shop floor with their serenity. Invariably, they are liked and respected by every member of staff.

All the same it's a good idea for supervisors to let their names and addresses be known to the police — just to be on the safe side.

The Cocky Approach

Electrical goods retailers have always been regarded as the aristocrats of the High Street, and rightly so.

Nowhere on the High Street is product knowledge so important; indeed it is quite often the difference between making a sale and making the sale of a similar item with a slightly different technical specification. This detailed knowledge of the technical fact sheets of their goods is the hallmark of their profession, so much so that they not only impart it to customers (regardless of whether or not their customer is within earshot) but also happily to each other.

When there is a scarcity of customers, you will hear them playfully trying to outdo each other, triumphantly shouting hard disk capacities and pixel resolutions to each other over the noise of their colleagues' jokes. How do they do it? How do these young sales people with their uneven skin, hair and education, manage to be lords of all they survey, to cut such a princely swathe. There's a simple answer, one from which all salespeople – from the humble shoeseller to the cultured dining ware retailer – can take a lesson: they embrace the power of cockiness.

Cockiness should not be confused with confidence, or urbanity, or professionalism — all anaemic versions of it. Cockiness is a joyous blast of swagger, a compelling, red-blooded force that creates a heady atmosphere of salesmanship throughout a shop and often onto the pavement beyond.

Too many shop assistants these days seem apologetic about the job they do. But why? The world, so it seems, is intent on spending its life buying, so selling is becoming more and more the most essential of the professions. People now believe they can buy their way to the perfect future that they desire, and we sales people stand at heaven's gate!

If you're not cocky, you should be! If you are already, then try throwing even more bravado into the reciting of those mobile phone tariffs.

The Honest Approach

Your customer has a broad back, long arms and an unnaturally small head, and she tells you she wants something that she'll look nice in at a wedding.

Quite honestly you're going to have your work cut out.

Inexperienced staff frequently believe they face a dilemma in situations such as this. If they fail to satisfy the customer's demands, the customer will believe that the store's range and styles are deficient. If they're honest with the customer and tell them that, given their spare parts physique, they've set the bar too high, the customer will feel grieved.

There's no dilemma. Customers come and go but your product line is with you forever. You cannot allow a customer to leave your shop with a poor opinion of your merchandise, especially when what they're looking for is more likely to be the realisation of a prayer than something with a product code.

You must be honest, and, in truth, customers appreciate honesty, if it is delivered with professional objectivity.

It is good practice to appraise a customer before they try

on any clothes, and quickly and clearly summarise their shortcomings — use a flat, clinical tone with no hint of sympathy or sadness. You should save any eyebrow-raising, sharp intakes of breath, or exhalations of despond until the customer is safely out of sight behind the changing room curtains.

If the customer queries any of your remarks, politely press them home. It is essential that you and the customer agree on the base you're starting from. Many customers will be unaware of their flaws, no-one ever having taken the trouble to point them out before, so expect a little resistance, and perhaps some tearfulness (women should be chivvied through this, men prefer to be left alone for a moment to recover their dignity).

Once over this though you'll find the customer more amenable to your suggestions and guidance. Often the customer will buy clothes they would previously have felt unhappy about wearing, but which now with their lowered expectations they're grateful to have found.

It should be pointed out that even using honesty properly, you cannot always expect such success stories. It may well be that you're unable to find merchandise suitable for a particular customer. Fortunately, in such an instance, the customer is now aware that this in no way reflects on your store.

A Little Additional Something

It is good retail practice to offer a customer making a purchase another product.

There is no need however to rack your brains for the perfect complement for their purchase; the suggestion doesn't necessarily have to be a sensible one. The important thing, as always, is that you have demonstrated your helpfulness. To signal to the customer that your suggestion is not to be taken seriously, it is usual to begin with, 'May I interest you in...?'

These days many retail establishments, such as railway station news-stands, make life easier for their staff by kindly providing an obviously unpalatable item to offer to customers, such as a fizzy drink or a roof-slate-sized bar of chocolate. Both staff and customer feel duty has been satisfied when the sales person asks, 'May I interest you in this month's special promotion, it normally retails for £1.30, but this month only we're selling it for 50 pence with any other purchase?' and the customer correctly answers, 'No'.

Coffee shops, as usual, have taken this simple courtesy and made it into a model of finesse. Go into any of the new High Street coffee shops and ask for a coffee and a pastry, and the assistant will unerringly respond: 'Can I get you anything to eat with that?' Masterly.

Amusing Customers

If you want your workplace to be a happy, sociable environment, it is important you make time throughout the day to see the funny side of life.

Sharing a joke or a divorce anecdote with colleagues will keep you all cheerful, but you should never forget that, in this as in so many other instances, your customers are your greatest resource.

Each customer is a trove of amusement. Enjoy them. If

there's anything funny about the customer you're serving – a nose piercing, a minor physical deformity, a shooting jacket, a visible impatience to be served – don't let it go by.

It would be uncivil, though, to find amusement in it in their presence. When they leave, however, where's the harm in sharing it with a colleague, or even better with the next customer you serve? He or she would have to be a curmudgeon not to laugh along with you in the ribbing of the previous customer.

On the same lines, if a previous customer has complained about some aspect of your store or service, when they leave the shop have the last word from that conversation with the new customer you're serving.

Remember, a customer doesn't want to hear the ins and outs of your previous conversation, just a précis of the main points, your gauge of the instability of the departed person, and finally and crucially that as a customer they are 'better than the last one'. The result: your customer, complimented, leaves with a spring in their step.

Remember to reply to their, 'Goodbye' with 'No problem' — to underline that *they* haven't been.

Warding off Burnout

People unfamiliar with the world of retail are often surprised to learn that a great number of employees who leave the profession claim to do so because of burnout. In fact, burnout as a reason for leaving is second only to 'don't know'.

Those more familiar with the trade recognise that the crucible of the shop floor, with its long periods of relative quiet and short sharp flurries of excitement, is not too different from the experience of combat as recounted by soldiers returning from war zones. The hardest bit is the waiting, they say. And so it is with the shopfloor.

If sales assistants are to stay in the profession and not join the exodus to other, less fulfilling, professions, they must learn to cope with long, stressful periods of boredom.

The best way of doing this is by utilising the now largely unfashionable method of transcendental meditation. Sit in a quiet place and, through the simple repetition of a phrase, allow your mind to switch off. In department stores, staff tend to use the hat department, though more and more it is becoming commonplace to find a small room off the shop floor. Occasionally there is criticism of the practice. It has been pointed out that outside of busy periods it is impossible to find any staff in department stores. This is patently true. But I would counter that if meditation were not available, it would be impossible to find staff even in the busy periods because the majority would have decamped to less stressful jobs.

If you work in a small shop it is not always possible – even with the best will in the world – to meditate off the shop floor. The following technique, however, can be just as effective and can be done sitting or standing on the shop floor.

Focus on a point ten to twenty yards away from yourself. Slow your breathing and continue to focus on your point, excluding all other thoughts. If your mind drifts, just stop your train of thought and return to concentrating on your focus point. After some minutes you'll find your mind emptying and your jaw will slowly begin to drop as your entire body slips into a state of complete relaxation.

It's possible to stay in this completely blank state of 'slack jaw' for several hours. Should someone speak to you, it takes only a minute or so to return to full consciousness.

Keeping Alert and Animated

In busier periods it is necessary to keep your mental faculties in a state of alertness, ready for any query with which the customer may surprise you.

If there are colleagues around you, it is a simple matter of creating conversations in which everyone will want to have a say. The Canary Islands, pet pregnancies, decorating, weather maps, train tariffs, relatives, tequila, dentists and wedding buffets are subjects that should be avoided – all are too provocative and invariably end in people overheating. Rather choose a safe subject such as religion or politics, neither of which will have any personal resonance for your colleagues. If you are not in company, it is still reassuringly easy to keep yourself alert.

Reading a book is one of the easiest and still, I think, one of the most graceful ways of keeping your mind tuned in and ready for a customer rush. It is best, though, not to let yourself become so engrossed in the book that you lose retail readiness. Try to get your hands on a good page-turner. The absence of character, adult emotion, intellect and humour in the authors of such novels guarantees that you'll never have more than a wafer-thin engagement with the book.

Also, chewing gum vigorously is an excellent way to keep mentally engaged. Originally an American habit, it is now mandatory for all Post Office counter staff.

Unnatural Demands

It can happen that the many hours of forecasting and logistical planning that go into stock control can be swept aside by irresponsible mentions of stock items in the press, or on radio and television. The demand created by such publicity requires supervisors to draw on all their resources to control it.

- Any items in demand at the front of store should be moved to the back of the store.

- Any items on display should be taken off display, put back in their original packaging and put on shelves below waist level.

- The window should be emptied of the items — and similar items which might suggest that you stock the advertised items.

- The staff should be briefed about the danger of inordinate demand and told to put on an expression of bewilderment whenever asked about the items.

- Only the most persistent customers should be directed to the items. Others should be sent to your competitor so that they run out of stock. If sales of the items continue despite these efforts then the items should be taken off the shop floor and hidden in the stockroom.

- If the demand continues and shows no sign of abating, the items should be returned to the shop floor and heavily discounted.

- If these sell out, then, after a cooling off period of three to four weeks, a small amount of stock should be reordered — no more than three or four days stock based on the items' rate of sale. The calculations for the rate of sale should include the period when the items were hidden in the stockroom, as they were in stock at that time.

- If these sell out, this can be taken as evidence of genuine, heavy demand. Monitor this customer demand for a fortnight and, if it continues, order enough stock to fulfil three months sales.

- When this stock fails to sell, return it to the distributor. At the next half-yearly management meeting, cite the failure of this stock to sell as an example of over-ordering and of the danger of knee-jerk responses to increased demand.

- Tell the staff to remove their expression of bewilderment when asked about the items.

Refunds and Exchanges

Just as we are happy to sell to our customers, so we must also be happy to refund or exchange their purchases should they require us to do so. Our highest priority is that we keep the customer happy.

Often the best approach is thought to be a no-questions-asked returns policy. This is a marvellously winning idea thought up by the top retailers. Nevertheless, while it may please the retailer, who can bask in the magnanimity of it, it is not very satisfactory for the customer.

Customers want to be asked questions. Whipping that toaster out of a customer's hand and thrusting another identical one in its place, may seem like a problem solved, but it has deprived the customer of an opportunity to tell their story: a story that they have most likely been rehearsing during the journey to your shop.

Whether it is Captain Scott's ill-fated expedition to the South Pole – pipped at the post by Amundsen with worse to come – or a toaster that refuses to pop up, failure makes a good story and the customer must be allowed to tell it in all its exhausting detail.

There is another count on which the no-questions policy falls down. If there is anything more exciting to describe than failure, it is success — tales of adversity overcome.

Where's the story to tell in walking into a shop and having your toaster replaced and receiving an apology and an ingratiating smile? Where's the battle of the Titans or the Athenian struggle which a customer can relate to their cheering friends, to their wide-eyed children, to their enraged internet forum? Where is the obstinate sales person who refuses point blank to refund or exchange the toaster, or even to discuss the matter? Without this opponent the whole return/exchange experience is a story fit only for spouses.

Give the customer a battle royal. Argue as though you mean it. And, when you're beaten by your superior opponent, have the courtesy to look absolutely infuriated.

Dealing with Old People

Treat old people as you would any other customer. These days senior citizens are as physically and mentally energetic as people half their age, and no longer need be patronised, shouted at or pointed out as a source of amusement.

Many now have incomes and so find themselves with tidy sums of money to spend. It is true that you have to work twice as hard to earn their money, as invariably all will have done price and feature comparisons on the internet or have an authoritative newspaper clipping folded

somewhere about their person, but the reward is frequently substantial: a healthy sale and sometimes a gap of at least two or three weeks before they return with their purchase, and their Tolkienesque narrative, for their cash refund.

The importance of old people to the High Street, however, lies not in their spending power – welcome as that quirky revenue stream is – but rather in their presence in stores outside the peak trading times. Were it not for the presence of old people many stores would be dispiritingly empty during the weekday mornings and afternoons. The abundance of old people milling about gives a gloss of activity to stores, encouraging younger customers to come in and shop.

As a sales person it is vital that you realise their role and importance and do not, as happens occasionally, herd them out of the shop.

Out of Stock Items

Under no circumstances give any indication when the item may be coming back into stock — no matter how politely the customer may press you.

Beware the customer who tries to lure you into committing yourself with bait such as: 'I'm in town again next Wednesday, do you think it will be in by then?' or 'I'll ring up later this week and check if it is back in shall I?' or the brilliantly teasing 'Not to worry. I'm sure it will come back into stock eventually'. Don't commit yourself, especially not to the binding notion that stock will arrive 'eventually'.

The mysteries of the supply chain are far beyond the understanding of all but one person or, at best, two people in your organisation. Some organisations even know who these people are. As a sales assistant though such things are beyond your ken. The most useful thing you can do in

such a situation is to help the customer to understand the essentially mystical nature of stock supply. The best way to do this is to reply to any stock replenishment query with a look of blank astonishment.

Only if the customer appears to be edging towards hysteria is it advisable to say a few words.

Dealing with Emotional Intelligence

One of the questions frequently asked by sales assistants is how to deal with emotional intelligence; that is, customers who think they are brighter than you and lose their temper when you refuse to acknowledge it.

Generally customers who have reached this pitch of pomposity and anger are impossible to pacify. It is unlikely that they are going to be persuaded back to a position of reasonableness. The only way to restore calm is to antagonise them further, and then a pinch or two more, so that eventually they storm out of the shop frothing with rage. If you have the time before they leave, don't forget to remind them that they can save ten per cent by joining your customer loyalty scheme. If you do this, they should, as they head for the door, vow never to return to the shop.

The downside of this approach is of course that you've lost a customer for perpetuity. The considerable upside is that you've gained a hoot of a complaint letter, bristling with wildly overwritten indignation.

It is worth pointing out that the ability to write an intelligent, well-structured letter of complaint is a skill on the wane as more and more people choose the telephone, or more rarely graffiti, as their preferred media of complaint, neither of which sadly can be thumb-tacked to a notice-board and wittily annotated.

Shoplifters

It is easy to see how some people could wrongly consider shoplifters to be the natural enemies of the sales assistant.

In fact, shoplifters and sales staff usually have a 'live and let live' attitude to one another. Shoplifters quietly take the goods they want and importantly – give or take a little cache or two – tend not to disrupt the stock.

Shop floor staff are not accountants and the fact that shoplifters do not make a contribution to profits for their goods is a small balance sheet detail that they are happy to overlook. Add to this, too, shoplifters' celebrated low maintenance (they never ask for their goods to be bagged, or if they're available in a lighter colour), and the case against shoplifters seems to weaken. I have heard the argument in staff rooms that in many ways shoplifters are the perfect customers. This is, of course, ridiculous. Though when you factor in the reduction in staff costs you could achieve if you didn't have to serve the people who take away your stock, the difference between customers and shoplifters as income streams is surprisingly small.

For a time it looked as though the delicate balance between sales assistant and shoplifter was about to be irreversibly disturbed. The new security personnel situated at the

entrance to stores were a deterrent to every sort of undesirable; it seemed inevitable that the shoplifter would be caught in their net. As so often happens, though, nature has its ways of restoring balance and it turned out that the security man on the door was there only to protect and woo that slight blonde girl on the front till.

However useful shoplifters are in keeping down stock levels it is wise not to be too friendly to them in case they take advantage of it and start cadging carrier bags from you.

Browsers

In no other commercial sector would anyone be tolerated who caused as much damage as browsers cause in retail establishments.

The advent of CCTV and short-wave radios has made it easier for shop staff to keep a track of browsers, and shops are now able to contain their depredations far more effectively than before. Nevertheless, they still present a serious threat to the orderliness of a store. If a store is to be successful, it has to control its browser element.

The newest and by far most successful method that has been devised is the 'firewall'. Despite its simplicity, it has proved surprisingly effective.

The firewall consists of two barriers, each designed to block a would-be browser.

The first barrier is at the entrance to the shop. A member of staff greets anyone who enters the shop as though they were an old friend whose name they cannot remember. This show of strained, uncomfortable friendship is often enough to repel those who foolishly thought they could just drift into the shop and look round.

Those who succeed in passing through this firewall are then approached by another member of staff. It is this sales assistant's job to ask the customer 'Do you need any help, today?' The message is clear. Previously, on another day, you took up precious staff time with your demands. It is futile to point out that this isn't true, that this is perhaps your first visit to the shop. The 'firewaller' makes no claim for factual accuracy. Rather the breezy tone of the remark cloaks a biting sarcasm that leaves teeth marks on even the most innocent of customers. Most people leave the store at this point. Only the most determined stay.

In stores that use the firewall method, customers as they make a purchase are asked, 'Has anyone helped you today?'

A customer who names a member of staff should be marked down as a browser, or a fraudster, even though he or she is making a purchase. Who else but someone involved in malpractice would remember the name of shop staff?

Experience Marketing

Windows are the Achilles' heel of the sales assistant.

Backed into a corner by a demanding customer, a sales assistant always has the escape route of telling the customer that the item they want is out of stock, or no longer made by the manufacturer or, best of all because it precludes any further discussion of supply, that it doesn't exist.

It takes great moral fibre, however, to deny the existence of an item when it is sitting on display in the window.

More often than not these days sales assistants lack this quality of moral fibre, though there are still a few of the diehard older generation of sales assistants ready to have a go, defiantly standing firm in the face of customer apoplexy.

Staff Breaks

Organising breaks is the most perilous and important job you may ever have to undertake.

It is, also, one of the few critical paths in retail, so it is imperative not to allow customers and their look-at-me waving to get in the way. Better to have one or two dozen harrumphing customers than a riot of staff fury.

Owing to the incendiary nature of this task, it is usually given to the member of staff with the highest muscle to fat ratio, regardless of gender. Or in the absence of any clear winners using this ratio, the highest fat to muscle.

New thinking, however, says that the task requires more brain than brawn.

To find suitable candidates, supervisors should listen to colleagues reflecting on celebrity marriages and the suitability of the partners. This is now considered the most accurate way of gauging intellectual acuity. More and more frequently now, this is how break organisers are chosen.

A colleague will cheerfully forgive you a sustained, physical assault, laughing it off with a these-things-happen-at-work generosity. Tinker with or forget their break, however, and

you can expect a period of Arctic frostiness towards you lasting between three years (no religious beliefs) and twelve (a Christian). Buddhists never forgive.

Sales

Now that most well run stores have sales that last for the greater part of the year, customers' over-excitement at the prospect of new, non-discounted goods can create problems.

The fast pace of non-discounted shopping takes many customers by surprise. Rather than strolling about a shop, gazing half-heartedly at the difficult-to-shift discounted goods, they now find themselves having to career about, looking at finite, disappearing stock, making split-second decisions whether or not to buy.

This increase in pace can be both exhilarating and scary. Nervous exhaustion is a common complaint. Heart attacks and hysteria are not uncommon. Arguments and stand-offs are an almost daily occurrence. Because of these problems many shops are now stepping back from even the few periods of non-discounted shopping they offer. Sensibly, even when there is no advertised sale, they are now leaving large tracts of their store filled with discounted and special promotion items. Our High Streets and shopping centres are saner, safer places because of it.

Christmas

When you are struggling to change the till roll in front of a queue of irate Christmas shoppers, it is important to remember that Christmas is not just about stoking the fires of consumerism, but also more importantly about celebrating the imminent birth of Christ in two to three months time.

This would be an easier task if Christmas were not such an onerous time for retailers.

The lion's share of a shop's annual income is earned in the last few months of the year before Christmas. Retailers and shop staff would prefer their sales to be spread evenly throughout the year and not to be so top heavy. This, they argue, would make life more pleasant for everyone.

Over the last decade, retailers have made monumental efforts to try and relieve the Christmas bottleneck.

They have tried to ease congestion by lengthening the Christmas sale period: decking the stores with festive decorations, playing carols and sleigh-bell classics earlier each year, as well as segueing Christmas with the Festivals of Light, the *Eid* festivals and the Back-to-School campaign. This has been a success of sorts. Many feel, possibly justifiably, that the public could have responded more enthusiastically to this clever initiative.

Another approach to relieve congestion has been to promote Easter more energetically. Easter is now not only a major religious feast but also the second best trading period of the year. Nevertheless, many retailers feel that Easter could be marketed more aggressively, increasing the range of the merchandise associated with it, making it more like Christmas.

The most ingenious idea, however, was thought up by a loose affiliation of retailers, poultry farmers and licensed

victuallers. Their plan was to create a third major religious holiday in July or August. Around this feast would be developed another extended shopping period. This idea has been heartily embraced by everyone in the retail trade.

Religious authorities, however, have been slow to react to the idea, displaying an indifference that has infuriated shop workers everywhere. Shop workers now feel angry at this lack of initiative, and increasingly anxious that each Christmas trading period will be more frenzied and ungovernable than the last. This utter hopelessness is apparent on the face of each and every sales assistant at Christmas — despite the Santa Claus hats and the other festive jollifications provided by management.

As things stand at the moment, you'd be hard pressed to find a shop worker in Britain who does not feel that the Church has let them down.

When It's Gone, It's Gone

Over the past few centuries, British customer service has proved itself remarkably resistant to change.

Nonetheless, there are powerful modern pressures on it. Burgeoning internet sales and the growing influence of the cheerful, featureless American model of service both, though from different directions, are encroaching on its territory.

Many shoppers prefer the convenience of shopping from their home, with its wider choice and frequently cheaper prices, and are deserting the High Street. Many stores now choose to cut corners and rather than take the longer, more arduous route of training staff in the British tradition choose the American fashion. A sales assistant can be trained in the American fashion in an hour, based as it is on the idea that you should always look like you're pleased to see the customer — an easy trick to pull off. The British tradition, using its customer mantra, *Remember, you know nothing about the customer,* would use that same hour to hypothesise about the social disorders and mental imbalances that a customer might conceivably possess.

It might be concluded then that perhaps we are witnessing the closing moments of British customer service as we know it.

Well, one need only walk around any shopping centre to know that this isn't so. Observe the new generation of sales assistants at work — many of them not even the children of shop workers, yet possessed of an intuitive understanding of the concepts of customer service that is as natural as it is pleasing. So long as they exist we can be assured that there is no lack of talent out of which to build the next generation of British sales assistants.

Yet, if they remain unappreciated, what incentive is there for these talented youngsters to stay in the profession? It may be that by our lack of appreciation we destroy a unique, irreplaceable part of our heritage.

This book, I hope, will have helped people move some way to understanding the basic principles of British customer service — and so aided its appreciation. In its modest way, I hope, also, that it will help people at last to recognise British customer service for what it clearly is: this country's most characteristic, and therefore possibly greatest, national treasure.